BATTLE
PLAN

BATTLE PLAN

PLAN

(REVOLUTIONARY POETRY & SHORT STORIES)

MWALIMU K. BOMANI BARUTI

ISBN: 0-9785531-1-X

Akoben House
P.O. Box 10786
Atlanta, Georgia 30310

www.AkobenHouse.com

Printed in the USA by
Morris Publishing
3212 East Highway 30
Kearney, NE 68847
800-650-7888

TO

Ayi Kwei Armah
Autum Ashante
Gwendolyn Brooks
Chinweizu
Mari Evans
Ngugi wa Thiong'o
Kenneth Zakee

Dedication

This collection is dedicated to the recorders of our stories, our philosophies, our aspirations, our inspirations, our Way.

Because we are the culmination of our way, this tradition, this spirit, these words have specific meaning to our mission and vision as Afrikans working to empower our people. Therefore, this collection is also dedicated to those who have yet been unable to record our thoughts. I hope these reflections give expression to what lies deep in the hearts of the many warriors necessarily too engrossed in their work to fritter away precious time jotting down their knowledge and wisdom on paper. I hope that those warriors who have been given the singular talent of writing and/or speaking our truth do not find my work too limited or amateurish. But, more than all, I hope this collection meets with our Ancestors' approval.

Acknowledgements

I humbly offer medasi pa to Odumankoma, the Abosom and the Nananom Nsamanfo for this creative opportunity. I give medasi to The Community for assisting us in our efforts to be independently Afrikan as without that this would not be. Of course, as with all of Afrikan worth that came from Spirit and pen before this, Yaa is the key to the uncompromised release of these words.

Table of Contents

Divide and Conquer 13

Betrayal 16

when I was a child 19

the time has come 29

with time 35

Patriots 38

Battle Plan 43

black islands, white sea 46

Frustration Denied 54

sesh 58

synthetics 60

To The Bone 62

overexposed 64

division of race labor 65

Resident Evil 68

In Passing 71

Reciprocity 73

Divide and Conquer

Our ancestors
& our enemies
cruise through our veins
engaged in historical battle
over our souls.
Our blood boils over.
There is no peace.
Combative traditions
of unrelenting
assault
& rebellion
fighting
to the death
haunt & define
our existence.

War rages
in our very soul.
War rages
that can only
be purged
by removing
the European
(or the Afrikan).
They will not stop.
We cannot.

There is no possibility
of compatibility.

Irreconcilable differences
remain irreconcilable.
There must be
division
& death
to regain
what *we* make
of life.

Annihilation/removal
is necessary
to regain
final,
total sanity
to achieve
an absolute,
defended
ReAfrikanization.
War is critical
to this end.

They say
we cannot kill
all
of our enemy.
That is only true
if
you allow
that enemy
to remain inside.

Only through a violent tearing
will our enemy
become one,
identifiably

divided from the Afrikan,
not two.
Only with
an active,
acting consciousness
can our energies
be directed
against our mothers' violators
against the savages
who have eternal,
supremacist designs
on Afrikan
ancestral rights
to our minds
our vision
our humane existence
as a solvent,
global nation.
Only then
will inner
& outer
peace conquer
ourselves
& our enemies.

Betrayal

every people
has weakness.
every weakness
has followers
who seek
to destroy
the people
they feel
have abandoned them
or never were them.
crossovers
are dependent
on the people's
perceived
level of vanquishment
(are they
winning or losing
not
whether they have
won or lost;
freedom is not free)
and
how long
they have been
lost/off their path.
weakness increases
with disbelief
in oneself
in one's people.

with time
weakness
converts
true disbelievers
some willing
some fearful
who can
easily
add up to
armies
over time.

WE
call true disbelievers
negroes
(among other things).

all true
revolutionary people
removed their
true disbelievers
before moving on
to destroy
the original sources
of their disbelief.

for negroes,
as for their allies
who work
against US,
there will be
no rest
here or after
because
they
reacted consciously.

they did not hedge
in their hatred.
soullessness
a desperate chaos
is an eternal sentence.
yurugu knows this.
you can
relinquish
your soul
for the love of others;
many have
for less.

the Universe
forever
keeps unforgiven
those
who knowingly
work
against its peace.

when I was a child

I was sheltered
from the violence.
I was sheltered
from this time and place.
I was kept safe
from My own curiosity
about a people and way
of real, obsessive hate,
kept home
under protective eyes
and cushioned
behind padded walls,
by a community
masking fear
and pretending rebellion.
Oblivious, I played,
played hard
in the arms
of an Afrika unrecognized,
in the spirit
and arms
of a people
and space
of natural, disciplined love
amid a clear vision
of dreams undeferred.

I expected
an honest world.

I expected
a morally clean
and ethically grounded
social reality,
a world
where individuals
used golden rules
to measure
their integrity
and godliness.
I expected
good
to overcome evil
of its own accord;
unwittingly,
I expected Ma'at.

I assumed
that life reflected art,
pure, original,
hand carved, ebony art.
I assumed
that one's eyes
must reveal
one's soul
because I was told
that humans
did not lie
to lie.

I believed
in the heart
and soul
of white people.
Even while
we joked

over their
absence of rhythm
and rhyme,
I still believed.
I believed
We were all human
in the heart,
all the same
under the skin,
all equally human.
I truly believed
in the spirit
of universoul brotherhood

I felt comforted
in the notion
of peace on earth
goodwill to all men.
I felt comforted
cradled in
the progression of
liberal/open-minded and civilizing
western ideas and machines.
I felt the comfort
of a stupor –
relaxed,
without care.
I felt eased in
being at home,
in this place made safe
by democracy's wars.
I made believe
that one day
I, too,
would fight
as one

of the few
the proud
government issue,
that one day
I, too,
would be allowed
to save them
from themselves
as Wesley and Denzel and Will
have been allowed
to pretend.
I felt comforted
by the pledges
of liberty and justice
for all.
I recited them
from My heart.

I experienced justice
in mason's and matlock's court
where we were
served and protected
even though
we had no
true representation
as judge, jury, defendant or victim.
All in all
I knew
that I was free
and they brave
even though
I understood neither
power nor courage.

I sensed sure direction
in my aspiration

to be honored
and loved by
a people
who
claimed humanity
and
allocated salvation.
I saw
insanity
as sanity.
I even sensed love
and emotional content
in their distance.
I sensed
that any change
toward them
was corrective
and life-giving.

I believed
in the sermons
and conditioned passivity
of those
calling us
from behind black & white
"dog collars"
to love our enemies
to forgive our enemies
to forget ourselves
and accept destruction,
to cling to belief
impossibly beyond ourselves,
to save ourselves
for otherworldly salvation.

I believed that

the self-denial
of righteous rage
begot power,
that abstinence
against correcting
historical wrongs
bespoke
a higher manhood.
I believed
they were trying
to save my soul
from itself.

I sought solace
in the arms
of negroes/negoettes,
lost souls
championing justice
for all [others].
Solace came from
the belief that
others' justice
would bring our justice
out of a staged fantasy
where a few bad
apples donned sheets
and ignorance of wickedness
was their only fault.
I sought solace
in the goodness
of isolated, deliberate,
nation-serving, individual
european *acts* of "kindness."

I bet my energy
on excellence.

I bet my sanity
on a victimizing socialization
promising an upward mobility
judged by merit.
I bet that
these managers of chaos
would not see me
for the way I was,
that they would be forced
through the brilliance of
my act
to at least
grant me
a privileged invisibility.
I bet
that I could become
colorlessly happy
or,
if all else failed,
a black and proud
favorite.

But, instead,
I was led
along a path
where I stumbled,
where i stumbled again,
and again and again and again and again
over the piles of lies
and contradictions
left in clear view.
i discovered
I was wrong,
dead wrong
about
my expectations

my assumptions
my beliefs
my comforts
my sensing
my securities
my bets
my self.

So i learned
to watch.
And i grew.
i studied our truth.
i found remembrance.
i cried.
i raged.
i mastered self.
i acted accordingly.

i discovered
that safety
and security
in a place
that fed
on my spirit's death
was illusionary.
i discovered
that an
unprepared, stunted
maturity
left me open
to attack
from within
and without.
i discovered
that spoilage
gave free passage

on new slave ships
and old brutalities.
i discovered
that death
is not life.

i realized
that the drive
of empty,
pale, smiling,
lipless, fearful,
powerless "people"
to masochistically sterilize themselves
was a conscious effort
to conceal
their manifest destiny
as carriers
of chaos
and disease.

i found
out why
lies were told;
i found out
about fairies' tails.
i learned
why i believed them.
i understood
i was not them
nor they i.
i had
no conception
of soullessness.
They embodied it.
i finally
recognized death

and learned
to live
without it.

the time has come

(A poem of apology and appreciation of Afrikan
women from Afrikan men)

the time has come
for us
to be men
in the tradition
of our ancestors

the time has come
for us
to forever
speak truth
of Afrikan women

you
carrying us on your backs
when we
could not
walk
talk
stand
look in your eyes
ashamed
angry
enraged
over a manhood
denied

carrying us on your minds
when we
would not
vent
correctly,
instead
reaching out to hit
and hurt
the ones we "love"
who love us
more
than
we could ever
possibly know
in our confusion

pimpin'
and playin'
you
to ourselves
for ourselves
and our enemies
romancing you
enticing you
possessing, perversely obsessing
your bodies
with words misinterpreted as love
  lies to access
  and violate
  your sacred gardens
  infecting your divine wombs
for the love of a momentary
  ejaculated passion
for the love of money
and an animal's reputation

reducing ourselves to
the Mandingoes
of others' imagination
against you
and for them

and
even worse
blindly lusting
after others' women
some even stooping
and bending
over forward
in their confused lust
of other males
and their own

the drunkenness
the drugs
the dead rage
the friends
the things
the excuses
the games of
placing self(ishness) first
family last

we have done wrong.
we know who we are.
we seek forgiveness.

there are no excuses
in
Afrikan manhood.
only righteous struggle
and correction

into
absolute respect
for
Afrikan womanhood.
all else flows
from this
universal
complementarity.

you breathe life into
what we build
keeping us connected.
you extend family.
you create community.
you give life.
you are love.

we know who you are.
you are the ones
who produced
legions of us,
who will bear legions more.
we ask that you
do not rear them in anger
at us
for our ignorance
and fear.
our daughters and sons
must become
great
warrior priests.
remain nurturers
mothers, sisters, daughters.
no Afrikan deserves
to die
alone

in hate.

there are no bitches
in this Afrikan house
no hoes, no heifers,
no sapphires, no chickenheads;
only queens
queen mothers
and queens in training.
we know who you are.

you are
our first divinities
  all comes through the womb
the first human
  proven as first fossil
    the genes through which
      humanity is traced
the Black madonnas
  immaculate in conception and grace
the matriarchy
  bloodlines through which we claim human rights
the breasts
  which feed us, give us life
the economy
  our sustaining relations to production
our spirituality
  the ties that bind us as family in peace
the Kandaces
  everywhere down through the ages
    royal warrior defenders of our way
first teacher
  patient in retelling ourstory
beautiful
  from blue black to eggshell
refined

turning mere walk into art form
enigmatic
  a mystery beyond male comprehension
proud
  with every reason to be
ever forgiving
  humbly righting relationships of worth
soft, gentle, tickled
  honorable qualities of any woman
without blemish.

the time has come
for us to be men
for you to become queens
in our thoughts, words and deeds.

with time
(for Yaa)

after
our vision
has been claimed
and made
a mission
without rival

after
our truest talents
are revealed
through
an honest striving
for independence

after
our differences
are understood
as complementarities
and not
oppositional forces

after
our imperfections
are discovered
and neutralized
and growth
does not induce chaos

after
our bodies
know each other
and want
has matured
into need

after
our children
have multiplied
far beyond
our immediate
genes

after
our wealth
becomes the family
we keep
in thought
word and deed

after
we continue moving
in the way
of warriors/healers
even as peers
retire in defeat

after
we measure
among true elders
being asked
permission
to speak

only after
we know
each other
in this way
does love come.

Patriots

we surpassed all
in camouflaging our
homes, yards, clothes, cars, offices, bodies, world
with an ol' glory
confused victims
glorify their smiling victimizers
in hope
of peace and love
in this place
in this time
we
more so than all others
express undying loyalty
hoping to stave off
an eternal bloodlust
their colors
in our homes
to ward off
demons within
in our yards
to avoid
identification by the state
on our clothes
to blend into
a uniform individuality
on our cars
to confuse
the killer blue lights
of blacks and whites

in our offices
to increase
a competitive negro advantage
on our bodies
to prostitute
our most personal space
in their world
to escape punishment
for being born great

our patriotism goes
beyond the crispus attuckses
beyond the dorie millers
beyond a host of black firsts
seconds servicing the pale supremacy
which sought/seeks
to kill the Afrikan gene
our patriotism has gone
beyond urging
our sons, fathers, brothers, nephews
to kill yellows, reds, browns and blacks
        even competing whites
for psychopathic destroyers
we renew
our vows of loyalty
with fresher and fresher sacrifices
fearfully responding to
the hateful, retaliatory envy of feminist politics
toward white male homosexual military domination
of them and, inadvertently, us
we renew
our vows of fidelity
with our daughters, mothers, sisters, nieces
pushing and allowing them
to lay down
their lives, their children, their sacred wombs

for alien men
coming under the rule of their alienated women

witness
the red, white and blue
discoloring domestic battlefields
as our children
young and old
make history
giving colors
for the first time
since our captivity
priority
over style
even putting gang colors
valiantly safeguarding barren turf
to shame

witness
our children
draping themselves in
the red blood
of other's ancestors
the white skin
of their enemies
the blue waters
of our middle passage
basking in mentacide
escalating their suicide
gloating over our genocide
again and again and again
buying flags, ribbons, tags, clothes, whatnots
good money after bad

witness their parents
desperately fighting

for the right
to redefine
submission as empowerment
insanity as consciousness
genocide as rebellion
european as Afrikan
fighting for the right
to win the lie
of being free
of feeling safe
in hell

witness
our wasted genius
our dogged search
for ways
to prove our worth
to others
alien
hateful
incomplete others
us begging the approval
of barbaric children
planning, wishing, thinking
"if i could only save one european
in battle
please, Lord, just one
i would be a hero
i would be visible
i could lay down my cross
be admitted into whiteness
become colorless
be loved as their own"
such determined genius
addicted to a deeper form of crack
called whiteness

sad.
so, so, sad.

Battle Plan

If we recognize
that Afrikans
cannot
be
who we are,
cannot
be
independent,
powerful,
ancestor lovin',
self-respecting,
self-determining
people/family/community/nation
in the presence
of europeans
(and the allies
they have created
among us
and others),
as victims of
white supremacy,
racist aggression,
individualistic spiritlessness,
universal lies,
mentacidal barbarities,
as captives
of a willful, insidious
anti-Afrikan
insanity

endemic to the chaos
of the western cultural wasteland;
if we recognize
that these foolish children,
that these people of the ice,
whatever they may be,
wherever they may have come from,
however human (*like manhood, womanhood,
ancestralship and civilization, a developed, qualitative
state of being; not a given*) they may appear,
cannot be
who they are
without
holding us/all others
in cultural bondage
and a state
of physical,
mental
and spiritual exploitation
(for they come back
into themselves
no matter
how
or how long
they are
isolated
from others
and their power);
then we
as conscious
intelligent beings
can but reach
one logical conclusion.
we cannot share
the same
space, time and truth.

we cannot coexist
in the same air,
on the same planet,
interpreting the same universe.
the differences are irreconcilable,
insurmountable, beyond reason.
historical logic
reveals no choice
for Afrikans
determined to rear
independent,
powerful,
ancestor lovin',
self-respecting,
self-determining
children.
genocide into whiteness
or
removal of whiteness.
that is the question.
so, ...why do we equivocate?
(as they escalate)
war is absolute.
there is only
victory
or vanquishment.

black islands, white sea

water lays
against earth
only slight
in depth.
earth
is deep.

earth molds
and contains
cupping
its turbulent
ward securely
against egotism
amorphism
and anonymity.
water has no form
without earth
no validation
no place to settle
or rest.
land holds
water
together
water serves earth.

land
can do
without
water.

land is life
with
or without
it.
and even though
water dominates
the surface
the superficial, delicate crust
it
cannot do
without
ground.
it would
run away
be broken up
into puddles
drops
an atomizing mist in space
without residence
or integrity.

water's power
is illusional.
it only appears
to kiss the horizon
as it is involuntarily
pulled up
answering to
the mass
of the sun
the moon
mars
solar winds
its own cradle's gravity
all centrifugal forces
forcing it to rise

to their occasion.

it supports life
as does soil, air and light.
it doesn't give it
alone.

white water
is foaming, frothy
rushing, restless
surface
water
water
abrasive
to the land.
still water
deep water
is clear
black.

no matter
how much
water moves
into or falls down
on the land
no matter how
the water's erosion
reveals
layers of earth
hidden
by time
and merciful deity
the land remains
constant.
the soils
may even become

blended differently
because
of water's
agitation
but it remains
land.
the deepest depths
the highest reaches
are marked/defined/held
by solid formation.

but confused by water
we do not see
this strength
this resilience
this indestructibility
this presence
a guess called science
claims to measure in time
because
we only see
the sea.
we only see
ourselves
as individuals
little black islands
in a big white sea.
we do not see
that we
are the land
that forms
this sea
that can shape
this sea
by just
slightly

shifting
our sands of
"black diamonds and blue pearls."
this sea
knows
and that is why
it constantly smashes, crashes, bashes
blindly rams its head
up against the land's
natural barriers (a child's retainers)
in a dogged effort
to convince the land
that it has power
that it has dominion
over it.

that sea
does not like
how volcanic roots
erupt more fertile
black islands
for they gain height
and strength
from inside
deep inside
the black earth
where water does little
but evaporate
they spill life
onto their recreated selves
life that has awaited
inside earth's womb
forever
to cover the new
with the old
so they grow

stronger and stronger
with the aged liquid rock
that forms them
anew
with each molten bath.
the deepest of
the old, rich earth
comes forth
above the sea
shoring them up
with layer
upon layer
upon layer
of warm black earth.
as worn, razed
grey islands
demoralized
from fighting
their traditions
and each other
so hard
to see
who would
stand highest
in the
sea of whiteness
await submersion
total submission
to it.
some even still
try sinking deeper faster
drowning themselves
in confused hope
that the sea
will rub off
on them

bleaching them
into one.

the sea is not land.

in time
these new islands
will see each other
on the horizon
towering above
the sea
and its
weathered
once earthen
individuals.

in time
these new islands
will come together
and know
their common being
redefining themselves
as continents
and then
planet.

in time
they will come
to know the sea
as a child
fighting for an identity
that cannot be had
without the shore
without the land's
discipline.

they will know
beneath the sea
they are one.

Frustration Denied

I often tire
of fighting
for a people
who believe
in their enemies
even more
than their enemies
believe in themselves.
It is not easy
to work
toward
the enlightenment
of a people
hell-bent
on destroying themselves
as a personal favor
to those
they seek validation through
and even a semblance
of conditional love
from,
a people determined
to live
with their murderers,
rapists,
diseducators,
destroyers,
to sleep with them,
to eat out of their plates

and off their floors.
We have
grown comfortable
in
the company
of death.
It is hard
to make a people understand
an innate evil
that thrives
on chaos
when they only recognize
that other's "truth."

It is not easy
to be Afrikan
in an anti-Afrikan reality.
It wears at you.
It tears at you.
It can make you question
the depth
of your sanity,
the purpose
of your mission.
It makes peace
nigh impossible.
But I
would rather die
a warrior
in service
to my ancestors
and descendants
than live
the lie
of a slave
fallen

to the unrelenting pressure
of europeans, negroes and lost souls
calling us
to commit treason
against the Creator.
Spirit
is what I answer to.
Spirit
is what strengthens me
through my weariness.

Struggle,
with vision,
produces resilience.
It creates power.
It brings a warrior's peace,
a peace that lies
only
on the battlefield of justice,
not the bed
of forgiveness
and forgetfulness...
forgiveness
will not cease
their destruction
and
if we forget
we will not
be able
to find our way home.
To be engaged in battle
when what the enemy has already done
to our souls,
minds,
bodies
should have made

any revolutionary thought
impossible
is how
I know
we have already won.
The Universe
does correct itself
(through us).
Ma'at is justice.

sesh

writing
> *is* discipline

writing
> *is* ritual

writing
> *is* rediscovery

writing
> *is* building

writing
> *is* oral, symbolic, deeply layered

writing
> *is* cleansing, elevating, empowering

writing
> *is* struggling
>> to plainly articulate a nation
>> to explain
>>> a people
>>>> at peace and war
>>>>> with ourselves
>>>>> to ourselves

writing
> *is* claiming
>> what is Afrikan
>> erasing what is not

writing
> *brings* definition
>> to ancestors
>> to Ma'at

                to Spirit
                to morality
                to circumstance
                to rage
                to opportunity
                to complementarity
                to healing
                to proximity
                        to our Way
writing
        is a mission
                statement

synthetics

as you are
and to the degree you are capable
you may take our architecture
and fabricate its essence;
you may imitate the religion
of our spirit;
you may claim our science
and make light fiction of it;
you may covet what you see of our form, our
        elegance, our shape
inserting plastic here and there to approximate;
you may steal our melanocytes and afterbirth
ingesting color to cure the cancer you receive from
        what gives all else life;
you may buy our artistic genius
and important these images into every room of your
        homes;
you may even bring us there in person
to more closely study minds which can master any
        reality;
you may acquire the mechanics of dressing, driving or
        jiving like us
cheating on tests measuring soul which you cannot
        possibly pass;
you may even go so far as to offer us your graven
        paper images
for an applause only you could believe is real;
but no matter your effort
no matter your mastery at imitation

no matter how heartfelt your mimicry
no matter your sadism or sycophancy
no matter your need to feel and be
you will never, ever, ever,
have our cool.

To The Bone

europeans are ugly
not because
of how they look
but because
of how they think
their rot
is *deep*
this is not
to say
they could not
be pretty
only that
their ugliness
is to the bone
marrow

their bastard
cultural offspring,
negroes
and less so
lost souls,
at times
are even uglier
though only superficially
because
superior disadvantaged ones
always surpass
their "betters" (cultural creators)
in self-destruction

their identity
remains tied
to a reactive rebelliousness
without changing
their institutionalized oppression
even as they die
at their own hands

europeans are ugly
because they know this
because they conspired
to inferiorize
and work to
commit genocide
against our entire race

there is no beauty
in their new humanity
only makeup
covering up
ugliness

overexposed

they desecrate
our sacred space
our vision
our view
our beliefs
with grey skin
dead cells
deeply deadened dermis
shells without substance
no spirit, no life, no rhythm, no pigment

why should we
have to bear
witness
to so much
dead skin?
why are we made
to feel unclean
because of its presence?

division of race labor

so caught up
in our individual
completion
in defining, preparing
and realizing
missions for
our selfish selfless self
we are unable
to see our mates'
complementary
devotion to
and participation in
the deeper vision

we are only
participant observers
though essential contributors
in *our* phenomenal
return home
we sometimes act
as if
she were not
our purpose
women
give birth
they are
the portal
men
only

provide and protect
women nurture life
men secure its sacred spaces

that is
the Afrikan way

creating community
requires family
family requires
men working
with women
parents working
with children and elders
children working
with ancestors

nothing individually done
to elevate self
overrides
elevation of nation
no personal purification
stands
without national purification
everything done individually
impacts the nation

we sometimes forgot
our place
in the circle
we sometimes think
we are
the circle

sometimes
we forget

what is
Afrikan
love

Resident Evil

we used to say
ofay, cracka,
paleface, yt
being stuck
in a minority status
of mind
seeing them
as powerful
potentially benevolent humans
without moral guidance
from us
confused victims
because
we felt
their open frustration
aggression
before its content
required
a formal
confusion
then assimilation

we now say
ice people, destroyers,
psychopathic racists,
born killers,
yurugu,
because we *know*
the history

of their spiritlessness
we see
freaks of nature
we know
that history
does not change
a thing's essence
it reveals it

we learned
simple lessons
uncovered by our scholars
too many to name
too many unnamed
who sacrificed all
to reach back
deep into
others'
and our
past
to explain the present
condition
of our negation
from the outside in
they studied
the genesis
and evolution
of
the problem

through them
we saw through
the few bad apples
into one
corrupted, seedless core
we learned

to see it
as them
not him or her
not the klan
or world health organization
but the nation
of shepherd kings
of greeks
of romans
of old and new
europeans
of caucasian beings

we now see
our mistake
as people of spirit
often too forgiving
for our children's good
we tried
to measure them
one by one
when they
were only one

In Passing

She was loud, very loud, as she cursed at him, all up in his face, calling him out of his name, all kinds of "niggas," "mothers" and "faggits." She was so close he could smell the fried eggs she had had with grits only an hour earlier; so close he could see decades of crack in her eyes, so close he could feel how hard she had worked to drag out her suicide. And all he had done was bump her, just barely. Skin touching shirt brushing blouse touching skin. He had apologized, said he was sorry, truly meant it. But it didn't seem to phase her. So he gave up, quietly saying, "That's why they call it an accident." That must have been his final mistake because she exploded, like unstable nitro. Loud, right to his face, on the third aisle of the supermarket. He didn't cringe. He just stood there, taking it, wave after wave of rage, frustration, powerlessness. She could not have known who he was. There was no outward indication. And he wasn't really at liberty to warn her, or explain. Wasn't his choice. Not that anyone would have believed him anyway. Not that she could have comprehended. She finished and turned away, snarling. The roll of her eyes sliced him in a practiced precision. And, try as he might, she heard him. Sensed it. Couldn't clearly make it out but she felt his lips move. "What'd you say you faggit ass punk!? I'll kick yo punk ass right here, right now!!" blasted through him in less than the three steps it took her to get almost close enough to kiss. " Just...my people, my people." She instinctively reacted, reaching, her last mistake. He shifted to the left. The very tip of her right finger's cragged air brushed nail barely grazed his cheek. Her skin touched his. No cloth shielded her this time. Nothing but skin to skin, electrical contact. He waited. Knowing. Concerned, as if for a newborn. She didn't know. She shuddered and twisted, writhing in unbearable pain, as ten thousand years of her people's history corrected her mind, her spirit, her soul. She knew who she was, what she had been before this life, this lie. She hadn't known he was a healer, an ancient one dispatched to release his people from this chaos. She hugged him, squeezing tightly, almost as if for dear life. Then went about her life's work.

Reciprocity

Great Granddaddy still talks about how Great Grandmama always said that science fiction was the window to the Yuro soul because it revealed the things they most feared others would do to them. She always pointed out how science fiction betrayed their conscious awareness of the evil, mean things that they had already done and continued to do to others. She believed it proved that they clearly knew themselves, no matter how well they feigned ignorance.

He never doubted her logic because she was a seer, a true prophet. It flowed through the blood of the women in her line. And, even though he grew perplexed over just how to do it, he occasionally did give some serious thought to her demand that we not allow them to do to the inhabitants of other planets what they had done to our people here. The only words she spoke that he truly questioned were her visions of an alien invasion.

Still, the probability of her prophecy faded with her passing. Without her voice's pressing insistence, Great Granddaddy was left to wonder if it all might have just been wishful dreaming. His wondering grew less and less with time, that is, until the Alkebu arrived.

Well before the Alkebu arrival people had already seen virtually every possible version of alien encounter imaginable. Now, with hindsight, we can remember that aliens tended to be portrayed as unfriendly types.

Most often those who teleported themselves or traveled light years in their fantastic flying machines to find this fertile planet were portrayed as evil creatures coming to wage war against humanity. Aliens were feared as invaders, coming unprovoked to our "peaceful" planet. Dispassionately and selfishly, they claimed our air, our bodies and other crucial resources as their own.

The usual reasons for these fears were pretty obvious to the imagination made paranoid. The media had nurtured a deep fear and hatred of others in their captive audiences for centuries. So deep and irrational was this fear and hatred, this xenophobia, that it was considered a part of the natural order. But, in truth and reality, the media's imagination did no more than mirror the overly aggressive reasoning and tactics of the family from whom its science fiction writers came. This is all they knew. So this is what they wrote.

Given this fantasizing mentality, the average alien, like the average Yuro, tended to believe that there was just not enough resources to go around. And, since they had expended so much time and energy finding and razing Earth, we humans had to go. It always came down to a war of the worlds.

All this alien vilification aided and abetted every script designed to portray Yuro heroes as innocents. It allowed them to gain our sympathy as victims of a deliberate and undeserved terrorism from above. In a reality of opposites, where there is evil, there must be good. So, in a response provoked by alien invaders, Yuros were simply desperately trying to defend themselves from a sure and painful death. And, as we had been led to believe, even if we were intentionally left alive by these otherworldly, soulless fortune hunters, eventually all humans would have to be reduced to slaves in a superior race's quest to colonize and master the Universe anyway.

Occasionally, however, extraterrestrials did come to the silver screen in peace. Sometimes fear or want or even desire drove them to escape an overpopulated planet, dying sun or their own slavery or, especially loss of individualism, under merciless, tyrannical overlords. In these cases, of course, they approached our civilization on bending knee, without power or demand. They just wanted a place to live in peace.

But, this time the "invasion" was real, even though Great Granddaddy had said it still didn't seem so. He said that witnessing the Alkebu craft arrive reminded him of being in a car accident. Reality decelerated into a dream-like state, where you could see all about but could do little if anything to change what was happening. The thought and action of those witnessing this superhistoric event were paralyzed, but not their sight. It just didn't seem real. Truthfully speaking, it was surreal. The world virtually stopped as thousands and thousands of seemingly weightless ships gently floated down through the atmosphere, three or four settling a few miles directly over each of this world's busiest and most populous megalopolises.

Each starship measured over eight miles across at its widest point and was nearly a half mile thick. The color and texture of the hulls was hard to describe because they changed. On clear days, the ships became translucent, barely visible. The sun's rays passed through them as if through air, carrying warmth and light as before. Neither were heavenly bodies obstructed on cloudless nights. City lights interfered with telescopic probes more than these atmospheric blemishes. Exquisitely chameleon-like, they mimicked any cloud formation as easily as smog, blending in whether the storm brought rain or snow. In fact, it seemed as if the clouds and their precipitation moved right through them. Regardless, we no longer questioned whether or not we were alone in the universe.

At first, we were afraid naturally, fearful from our imaginings about the unknown. The basket-like protrusions extending downward from the center of each ship frightened us most. They resembled the horrendous weapons of war manufactured by our science fiction.

We tried contact. Nothing we had imagined, amplified music, light shows, white flags, whale sounds, nothing elicited a response. Curiosity gradually turned into frustration and, then, fairly quickly, into anger. "How dare they ignore us," arrogant politicians barked. "This is our land!"

Unlike in silver screen fantasies, though, the Yuro elite launched the first strike. Against protests from those of us who refused to succumb to irrational fears, the panic brought on by the Yuro's imagination compelled them to hurl the most destructive missiles on hand at them. The first wave went straight through the crafts, just like the sunlight and rain. The next were set to explode in the same airspace the craft occupied. They had no visible effect either. We waited. Still, no response came. Not even a respectful gesture of retaliation followed. Nothing occurred to momentarily unite all of us together against them. Nothing rained down on us that could have been used to temporarily distract the oppressed into joining forces with their oppressors.

Later, with the childish insolence of repetitive, habitual, manipulative liars, the Yuros offered up apologies, which fell on seemingly deaf ears. For still, no one, nothing from above, acknowledged our existence. With hindsight, there was really no need for the aliens to react. Their ships weren't even scratched by the Yuro's death dealing toys. We wondered if they had even felt the impact. The nuclear fallout from the missiles hurt us more than their explosive impact appeared to damage the alien craft.

Time made us less fearful, more comfortable, with the oval shaped bodies suspended above us. The ships were constants above their eyes, remaining motionless above the normal visual field, out of sight, out of mind. Most easily adjusted. Some of us even came to forgot their presence, in the way dutiful humans have been socialized to become when answers are not forthcoming or fear becomes too great a companion to bear.

The determined among us thought they were dormant, either full of corpses set out on a failed mission of conquest or cocoon-like pods waiting for the signal to rain down destruction on us. Religious zealots could not pass up the opportunity to either foretell impending mass destruction, except we be saved by them, or led congregations in worship of their newfound ovoid gods. Either way, pockets were lined with the currency of exploited fears.

Probes came back empty-handed. Passengers of helicopters that flew around inside the space occupied by the ships had no strange feelings or supernatural experience to report. Unable to acquire any meaningful data beyond their dimensions, but not wanting to be left out of the debate, the scientific community concluded that the craft contained amorphous, shape-shifting, complex life forms. From nothing, no data, no evidence, not even any decent hypotheses, they scientifically concluded that these life forms only wished to live undisturbed among the clouds thriving off of whatever nutrients they could extract from the thin air.

Even though it was known that both living tissue and dense objects could fly through them, airlines had taken the precaution of modifying their urban flight patterns around the crafts. Traffic and police copters lowered their altitudes without altering their missions. We had successfully adjusted to their presence. Our guests above no longer meaningfully affected life around us, negatively or otherwise. They even lost their edge as an irritating distraction. News of them became old, boring, almost forgotten.

The ways of this world settled back into what had been normal. Only fools and eternal optimists imagined that the controlled chaos of everyday life on Earth could permanently cease merely because we had company. After a while company are no longer guests and normal ways of speaking and behaving return. The unity between peoples fostered by fear dissipated. The casual disrespect and sadism that the streets, homes and places of work and play had grudgingly abandoned returned unchanged. In fact, it was worse than before because of the drive to catch up with the progressive regression that would have naturally occurred. "We're all human" slogans faded again into obscurity, taking the fake smiles and conversations with them. A once familiar distrust returned.

The vulgar slang of those well schooled in the barbarities of the Yuro mind returned to the popular media, obliging young voices to affectionately call the craft's downward protrusions "sky tits." Our youth, perverted by the insanities of a debased world, coined this endearing term. Those short, cylindrical cups protruding downward from the ship's centers, originally declared weapons of mass destruction, resembled a woman's detached breast. So many of the young had been brought up caged in sterile, motherless, state institutions that they unconsciously saw as symbolic of the mothers they never had. Nearly a century earlier "crack" had only been the beginning of the Yuro's scientific efforts to denurture the nature of Nukemba mothers, while "crystal meth" had escalated the already widespread distance of Yuro mothers.

For a while, the children's music played to the fantasy of a mother's healing milk, instead of sweetened chemical substances, coming from the "nipples." A large cult appeared worshiping the divine breast goddess. "Amniotic," a clear pitch black designer drug that made you feel like you were comfortably curled up in your mother's womb, floating in amniotic fluid, was concocted in basement labs and introduced to celebrate the fantasy.

Adults, on the other hand, generally concluded that these vessels, like our exploratory probes into outer space, were tools designed to study life here and not weapons bringing apocalyptic destruction. Fear faded to indifference. Indifference became forgetfulness.

On the last day of the seventieth year of their arrival they acknowledged our presence. Egg shaped, school bus sized craft appeared to ooze out of the sides of the motherships. They gently descended and landed on the front lawns of local and national capitol buildings all over the world. Remembering the uselessness of our weapons against the motherships, and still in fear of retaliation, no weapons were openly brought in to greet them. Upon landing envoys of nine Alkebu representatives exited the eggs. Not much later, they were ceremoniously escorted as honored guests into the homes of the world's royalty. No formality was spared. Although they had yet to utter a word beyond "greetings," the guests appeared impressed with the reception and accommodations.

Only the dispossessed, envious nations of color protested the absence of an extraterrestrial presence over their cities and at their welcoming feasts. Again, they found themselves floundering on the periphery of power. Of course, none of the chosen nations saw a need to empathize with them. For no country, except those most closely allied with and judged as part of the most technologically advanced world, had been favored with entourages of space shuttles. Because they sat at the center of that technologically advanced world, the Yuro community was ecstatic. It was indeed a gratifying and rewarding day for them. Centuries of creating a world of the "fittest" was at last being validated by apparent superiors. The game remained in their court leaving them still in the power position to explain this reality to our guests.

As they began to communicate, the Alkebu made it known that they had logically sought out the world's true leaders to break bread with and communicate their wishes. What better evidence, the Yuros thought, of the superiority of what they knew others, lesser humans, enviously called disorder. What better evidence could be given of the supremacy of Yuro definitions of universal culture, of the advantages of imperialist Yuro-style progress, of the supremacist way of those blessed with pale skin. Validation by obviously superior aliens quickly replaced the flattery long given by those who in awe of their magnificence had given them through imitation. Hedonistic celebration and self-aggrandizement became the order of the day. Secretly, many believed in the prophecy that aliens would one day come and exchange advanced medical technology in exchange for the reenslavement of Nukembas on their lesser developed worlds' plantations. The heads of Yuro governments had long ago secretly decided in favor of that scenario.

Everything went pretty much as expected. I guess the one shock science fiction had not prepared us for, except maybe by inference in the movie *Brother From Another Planet*, was the Alkebu's appearance. They were all very, very dark in color, a midnight blue black to a deep dark, purplish black. Their skin was smooth, without blemish and absent of makeup. Being barefoot, we could see that even the bottom of their feet and palms of their hands were the same color as the rest of their skin. Their hair was tightly curled and shiny, mostly fashioned in styles reminiscent of those sported by Nukembas of old, with women having the longest, more intricate, twisted styles. Their noses were quite broad and their thick lips often opened to reveal rows of crystal clear teeth which vibrated when they spoke. The white robes they wore, modestly decorated with various forms of symbolic writing, accentuated their well-rounded buttocks. The women were wider than the men and had ample bosoms. They were a tall people. Not one stood less than seven feet, a result, we later learned, of their home planet's lesser gravity. Most resembled the stature and appearance of one of the ancestral Nukemba tribes my family reverently called the Ancient Ones.

From their statements we learned that the visitors also had a racial history. It was a much more ancient one scarred by more intense war and conflict. In the beginning, their planet's environment had also provided distinct environments where its two dominant races had developed two irreconcilable realities in what their scientists called the "two nurseries."

Like ours, these two separate cultural nurseries had also produced two incompatible cultural personalities, permanently infused in the biocultural genes of people who had grown far apart in their social predispositions and spiritual orientations. In the more plentiful, warmer South, the Alkebu personality evolved emphasizing principles of creation and nurturance. The Greys, in the cooler, much less abundant North, were nurtured into a selfish and destructive predisposition.

Unlike here, though, there was no middle ground to confuse the racial, cultural differences. There was no zone of cultural confluence or blending where cultures met and evolved new ones. There was only one long battleline where wars were waged and none peacefully crossed. The Alkebu knew who the Grey were and had no desire to pollute their genetic code. Extremely limited amalgamation had occurred over the centuries of hostilities, so friend knew friend and foe knew foe, on sight.

The Alkebus eventually won the war of the races, crediting their success to learning early on about the natural amoral political treachery and lies of those who sought to destroy them. Their advantage was in never succumbing to the notion that liars eventually feel compelled to speak truth. They neither compromised their heritage nor desired integration with others they considered to be innately without spirit or a sense of morality. They had always been the dominant people on their planet, a dominance they came to realize was required to maintain and insure a balance favoring their race's creative side. But they had never felt compelled to institute an ideology of Black supremacy or racist laws to defend themselves from their own fears. They were old enough to know that unrestrained injustice against the disempowered always foments resentment and rebellion.

The Greys, however, could not live without oppressing others. They had been without power for so long that they could imagine no other way to feel alive. They couldn't even live in peace amongst themselves. And attempts by the Alkebu to dissipate the Greys' confusion by integrating them into the Alkebu's spiritually ordered reality, at least marginally, did not work. The Greys were like a virus, eating away at the Alkebu immune system. Eventually, the Alkebu found that they could no longer afford the growing discord or tolerate the debilities of their own liberal, wrongly guilty consciences. The Greys were just too conflictive. Even when they were kept locked away from everybody else for centuries, they returned to their way as soon as contact presented the opportunity. Survival of the species forced the Alkebu to institute a tough love that relegated the less fit, pigmentless citizens to subterranean mines. The Greys' mass removal from civil society took almost three generations of counter deceit and violence. But, once it was complete, it even became accepted as natural by the Greys, given their full realization that the darkness of the caves absorbed what little melanin they felt they had been cursed with. However, even this was not the end, for evil forced into isolation consumes itself. In their mad search for an ordered chaos, the Greys destroyed themselves. The Alkebu had come to the same conclusion that Earth's Nukemba scholars of old had. Evil must spread to feed. And, once spread to its outer limits, it returns with a vengeance to consume itself.

The Alkebu went out of their way to show that they best related to groups who had overcome similar problems here. Like their newfound friends, Yuros also felt more at ease in the company of like minds. Preponderant power and like-mindedness made for colorless relations. Surprisingly, the glaring differences in complexion, build and features posed no obstacle to negotiations. The Yuro's only fear was that the Alkebu might feel compelled to exact revenge for what they had done to Nukembas and other people of color here. There was the nagging question about whether the Alkebu secretly saw Nukembas as family.

They were reminded of the questions about loyalty to Yuroland by Nukemba citizens that came up nearly a century ago when they decided to use them as frontline soldiers in their final military conquest of Nkembaland. But, as they had been wrong about the suicidally patriotic Nukemba soldiers used in those wars against their own sisters and brothers, their fears about the Alkebu were completely unfounded. The aliens' deliberate refusal to communicate with any people of color, excepting those the Yuros had accepted as allies who were respected for their nationalism and power, astonished and impressed the mind of most Yuros. Some even found it amusing because it was like watching well heeled clowns pretending to be independent, thinking men and women in academic and corporate settings. Promises of a near future mating of Yuro and Alkebu royalty satisfied any remaining public questions about treachery on their part.

After months of friendly negotiations, Earth's chosen people agreed to share some of their most sophisticated technical skills with their guests in a good faith effort to further a burgeoning trust. Military experts paraded what they felt safe enough to share from their arsenals. History kept them cautious. To haphazardly reveal one's armament to the vanguard of forces possibly bent on invasion, no matter how impenetrable their craft or generous their friendship, did not seem like a good idea. Plus, for seasoned liars, the Alkebus' public denial of ulterior motives made little difference. Their intent was still privately questioned in many a distrusting Yuro mind. That would not change. Minds suspicious of themselves find trusting others impossible. As cautious as they were, though, the technology "show and tell" revealed much of their material advancements over the last decade or so.

But, of course, Yuros had never done anything without seeking to selfishly benefit themselves. They had their eye on speed and size. It was believed that the Alkebu could instantaneously transport themselves between galaxies and backward and forward within time. And the Alkebu had even more to offer. They surpassed humanity hands down in their ability to build things large. Even if they had not admitted to these technologies, their mastery of rapid space travel was evident by the sheer magnitude of their ships, as well as the stories of faraway spouses and recent offspring. Further, it was impossible for them to be indigenous to our solar system because we had fully explored all of the planets, and the closest sun with habitable planets was five light years away.

Years of open visits to the alien spacecraft convinced the Yuros that there were no weapons systems on board. How unusual, they thought. Never had they imagined a people so much alike but dislike them. Even knowing that they had taken up arms to reestablish internal order and defend against invaders, aggression seemed unnatural, even alien, to them. The nine years of talks and socializing fully confirmed that assumption. Yet, still, it took a long time and enormous effort for Yuro and Alkebu to become comfortable with each other. Negotiating delicate, often incompatible, cultural differences required much diplomacy and time.

All those years we had been waiting for them to reveal a hidden agenda, the Alkebu had been closely studying us too. They had been trying to determine which of this planet's groups was the most technologically advanced. Everywhere they had traveled in the Universe, they first identified and then approached the best technological minds to solicit their help in solving the developmental problems of their home planet. Strange as it may sound from looking at their spacecraft, they did not have the mechanical inclination or aptitude to produce weapons of war powerful enough to repel their all too frequently invading neighbors. Their culture was faulted with not having taken the centuries required to develop a proficient defensive or offensive weapons program. Something in their genetic makeup prevented this sphere of thinking to sufficiently develop. A communications systems that could detect incoming hostile forces before they entered their atmospheres was also conspicuously missing. The Yuros also came to realize that most of their mechanical technology had been borrowed and then modified to suit their needs. They had almost no talent for destruction. The Alkebu willingly admitted this flaw and now sought the council of the most powerful nations on this planet, as they had already done on others.

They had already studied us enough to distinguish predator from prey cultures. This they could easily do, and had done, from the air. Simply following the physical flow of resources and the trails of waste and impoverishment revealed the current locus of power in Earth's world order. Still, they were quite aware of how rapidly and capriciously global politics could change. They had been fooled before by superficial arrangements and exercises of power. They had been fooled by powerless people acting on behalf of powerful ones. And they had history, too. A balanced, tested proof only came from the historical record, from chronologies of the military campaigns that had led to the expansion and preservation of western global dominance. They needed to tap into this information base also.

But they also needed to delve more deeply into the cultural personality behind these exploits to know whether the patterns of aggressions were motivated by fear, or hatred, or both. They needed a holistic explanation. And, that could not be studied from above, for their victims had come to imitate their aggressors so well, and time had made it difficult to tell one from the other.

Aware of the Alkebu inquiry, and wishing to gain a decisive advantage in the competition for Alkebu technology, Yuros initiated their own information blitz. The Alkebus were supplied with libraries upon libraries of their interpretation of history. Their true color, or lack thereof, showed through most brilliantly in their campaign to demonstrate that they, above any other people, could be the most destructive and violent. Through this, they hoped to prove that they, and they alone, deserved to be awarded control over Alkebu technologies.

The alien's awe at their uncontested claims to martial superiority was obvious. And the Yuro's own egomania drew them into bragging about their real, not politically safe, actions and heroes. They stripped away the lies about the necessary but disagreeable obligations of their manifest destiny and openly called themselves imperialists. They made their evil shine.

They proved themselves a globally dispersed people acting as one nation. And they gloated over how they had others believe otherwise.

The theory of a few bad apples was quickly dumped for one of a few good ones. Everything from chemical to nuclear weapons, from Columbus to Leopold to Hitler, from the World Health Organization to Planned Parenthood to the CIA was laid open for the aliens to see how efficient and effective the instruments of their insatiable greed and genocidal aggressions could be. Conspiracies became uncontested fact with the documentation eagerly supplied by living conspirators and the children of former ones. They bragged about their genius at consistently piling lie on top of lie and having their enemies and victims fall for them again and again and again. It was other people's gullible ignorance, their tortured submission, not their excessive, inordinate aggressions, that was at fault, they argued.

They admitted to originating germ warfare and brazenly traced their use of it from long before the Native Americans, where they used disease-ridden blankets and their victims' sense of humanity to exterminate thousands, to its experimental use on the poor as well as the many millions held captive behind bars in their societies and oppressed in viciously exploited, neocolonized countries.

One of their most surprising revelations was to concede that they were the natural carriers of so many of the unnatural diseases which attacked and decimated hundreds of thousands of indigenous people around the world. Generations of Yuros, having developed high tolerances for the disease which the filth they were bred in brought, became the very carriers of these diseases. Other peoples, who did not thrive in squalor or otherwise unsanitary conditions, whether they had lived in the city or rural areas, did not develop these immunities because they were not exposed to compounded disease due to living in healthy, sanitary environments. These innocents naturally contracted the Yuro's diseases upon contact with them.

It was a most telling fact that Europeans knowingly spread diseases that passed from one human to the next everywhere they went around the world. They also kept secret their knowledge that they had contracted no harmful diseases from others anywhere which were not a part of the natural collection of diseases that everyone, whether living in rich or impoverished environments, was prone to. Sure, they had contracted diseases from certain plants and animals, but not other humans.

They also produced medical history records showing that they knew full well that before them there had been no plagues brought about by unsanitary complications of manmade environments. Suddenly diseased rats, flies, mosquitoes, rabid dogs and even the monkeys they manufactured to carry their lies became their children, offspring of the science and ignorance of their culture. Stories like "The Pied Piper of Hamelin" became recognized for the real historical records that they were.

Unknown to most, this had all been very well documented. They had only hidden it from others. Careful records had always been kept and great care had been taken to make sure that those records were passed only from one loyalist's hands to the next. Yuros even went so far as to admit to the genocidal motivation behind trying to turn entire populations into expendable drug addicts and initiating confusion and wars if they rebelled.

The number of Nukembas killed in the slave

trade suddenly jumped even higher than the nearly three hundred million exposed by Nukemba scholars who the Yuro's grandfathers had conspiratorially and nonchalantly dismissed as instigators of racial disharmony or as unnecessarily hypercritical of those benevolent Yuros burdened with civilizing a backward continent. They even admitted to having ended the intellectual rebellion of Nukemba warrior scholars either through buying them, isolating them from their people or publicly ridiculing them into effective silence. They admitted that they were aware that this was a calculated political effort, designed to make any further organized, rigorously researched accusations by new, disgruntled members of a new Nukemba vanguard impossible. They accepted responsibility for sabotaging every phase of the Nukemban centered grassroots movement, including all efforts to gain reparations.

The confession that they had grossly inflated the numbers of Yuros killed by others or other Yuros came as the great surprise, especially the numbers of their own who claimed to be murdered by other Yuros in their second official war against the world. An even greater surprise was their confession that these officially declared wars were simply civil wars that were no more than in house fights over who would control nonYuro resources and that they were clearly aware that they had been waging war against all other people since they first came to recognize themselves as a people.

Shamelessly, they bragged about those peoples they had permanently removed from the planet, of whom there were no more and who, even with their God-vying biogenetic science, could be no more, ever again. Further studies were made to calculate the stupendous number of individuals they had systematically exterminated everywhere they had set foot since their descent from the Yuros Mountains to conclusively establish their preeminent killer instinct. As the number murdered climbed higher and higher, so did the list of atrocities. The only question that still concerned the Alkebu was which came first, the killer instinct or hatred. They needed it to be the former.

The Yuro's victims had long ago come to the logical conclusion that nothing except sheer psychopathic hatred could explain their history of fanatical outward aggression. But their voices could no longer be heard above the roar of the Yuro boasting. They hoped against hope that the Alkebus would see it the same way, but held very serious doubts that these people, who were blacker than night, would ever become their allies. They could already feel their oppression under the Yuros deepening.

Sometimes, when my father replays this story for me, his face sort of glazes over. He refuses to admit that the pain is too much to bear. But I can tell. Each time he goes over this narrative he speaks as if on a mission to save my very soul. He will sigh, slowly shaking a lowered head and sternly demand, almost as if in apology for having to be so brutal, that I grasp the magnitude of the scores of Yuro atrocities so I can never feel secure enough to be lulled into the forgetfulness that still captivates so many of my kind.

A painful sadness fills Mama's explanations, too. I can sense her disbelief that such an evil people could have ever existed in the Universe. She cries when she tries to explain how Nukembas could have, for so long, confused the Yuro's wickedness as the rightful wrath of our Creator against our backwardness.

Surprisingly, most Yuro scholars also openly conceded the historical inability of their own to even

91

get along with themselves. In fact, a state of perpetual war had raged among them in their own fatherland as far back as their memories could carry them. It had been the testing ground for the violence and bloodshed they escalated when it was exported to others.

This confession included acknowledging their efforts to universalize their peculiar excessive violence and aggression in order to pass off their abnormality as everyone's. Along with this, the old habit of attributing innate causes to genetic faults, rationales that always lay beyond their control or character, was even pushed here. Their abnormality became the norm for all people. To please the Alkebu, they even devised scientific proof of their increasingly excessive violence and aggression as grounded in a natural, evolutionary survival of the fittest philosophy in order to prove that they, being by far the most violent and aggressive, dominated the top of the hierarchy of human progress.

It was an incredible turn of political events. For even the numerous Nukemba scholars who rigorously argued that Yuros unconsciously spread their excessively violent and aggressive behaviors beyond their borders in order to keep from imploding were given overwhelming support. Yet, only some of these previously defamed Nukemba scholars were elevated to the honored position of true scientists and visionaries. In their usual predatory fashion, Yuros took credit for most of the arguments made by others, proving they needed to vent their frustrations against others to insure that they did not obliterate themselves in fits of uncontrollable rage. The fact that they could economically and psychologically profit from others' stress and strife, through a chaos exported, fueled and subsidized by them, was given equal importance.

They admitted all this and more, confirming things many conspiracists had yet to imagine.

The clincher for the Alkebu was the Yuro's prowess in the air, for they had already shot down and warehoused a number of UFOs's that, incidentally, belonged to the enemy the Alkebu needed help defending themselves from.

The Yuro community intuitively grasped their and the Alkebu's needs. It would be no hardship for them to volunteer a moderate collection of their best scientific and military minds for a decade or so in exchange for technologies of speed and large scale construction. They made it known that it would be no problem at all. They could already taste the wealth of the stars. Shows like *Star Wars*, *Star Trek*, *2001: A Space Odyssey*, *Outland*, *Alien*, *The Terminator*, *Dune* and a whole host of sequels and others had at least mentally prepared them well for this eventuality. Combining the alien's space travel oriented technologies with theirs, especially the military component, would surely advance the conquest and colonization of their rightful share of the universe. As Great Grandmama had lamented, they had waited so long to contemptuously finish off this nearly depleted planet's scarce resources and move on to ravage others.

But that final assault against civilization everywhere would have to wait because the Alkebu did not simply want their technology. They needed the technological "genius" guiding the Yuro mind. They needed a technology that would grow, generation upon generation, indefinitely adapting to their changing needs, needs that they would never willingly soil their hands or minds with, needs that to their memory had always been and would always be. Military priorities, although pressing, were considered too savage, too barbaric, too far beneath them. They were the proper domain of the masters of crushing and unrelenting death and devastation, of warmongers and a culture that naturally produced serial killers and psychopathic supremacist groups. It required the mind of a people who instinctively turned everything, no matter how small or unrelated, into a weapon.

The Alkebu considered themselves a peaceful, civilized race, more than willing to admit the fault of being above violence. Technological advances in this area were beyond their natural abilities. They admitted to an extremely limited study of war. They accepted their role as peace mongers, all the while recognizing that there were others in the Universe who were not. And, to solve this problem, to the Yuro's chagrin, they were willing and able to physically transport the community of humans possessing these special skills from here to their planet as skilled labor. This, they finally made known at the last Intergalactic World Conference. They had found what they had searched centuries for – a truly evil genius. To take some Yuros would only create morale problems in the long run. So, from the beginning, they had prepared to take them all.

By the time the "chosen people" realized the Alkebu's intent it was too late. They were already being collected. Whatever the case, as the story goes, the Alkebu really didn't have any military power the Yuros could identify. So they felt no threat. That made them careless. But our guests did have a secret, undetectable weapon. They had mastered the art of mind control. Or rather, they had learned how to override the brain's instructions to the nervous and muscular systems by telepathically communicating with the pineal gland, regardless of how calcified it had become. They were advanced enough to know it was the center of the mind's spiritual power. Telepathically manipulating the pineal gland forced the human body, regardless of the mind's will, to carry itself wherever the Alkebu wanted it to go. Yuros did not have the intellect to develop a defense for this. They were powerless to defend themselves.

That was the Alkebu's strength. They could force your body to do their bidding, go wherever they wanted you to. It made no difference whether you were fully aware that your body was working against your mind. You were unable to do anything about it. And, interestingly, the more a people had their spiritual needs satisfied by the body, the baser desires, the easier it was for the Alkebus to control their pineal connection. Ironically, this phenomenon yielded an unexpected consequence. The so-called men of God in Yuro society were the easiest to control.

It was then that we discovered why the Yuro's missiles had been totally ineffective against the Alkebu ships. Mind control had been there from the beginning. The missiles had never come near them. Those who were responsible for pushing the buttons to launch them had been led to miscalculate their course. And onlookers were instructed to see them on course. The warheads had never posed a danger to the spacecraft. They had simply bypassed them and exploded in the outer atmosphere.

Scary, powerful stuff. The stuff mesmerizing science fiction used to be made of. They just landed the motherships outside the suburbs and had all the Yuros march into the holds where they already had bins filled with three months worth of stored goods. It only took a few months to round the entire population up.

It was only when they uncloaked their ships that

we were able to really see them. We could now clearly see their solid oblong shapes. Long pointy appendages pointed out in every direction from virtually everywhere on its surface of these rounded cylinders, like the pricks of a frightened blowfish. Wherever there weren't pricks, there were windows. There seemed to be millions of them. But what drew our attention and memories most were the ships' colors. They were mostly black with large red and green symbols all over. The Alkebu said these were the colors of their national flag, an ourstorical flag that kept them conscious of their love of their land and each other, a flag which had been created out of a deep reverence for the hundreds of millions of ancestors who lost their physical essences in battle to save their planet from the Greys.

But even after the history and the conditions and purpose of the relocation were revealed, some who were not chosen were not pleased. The sad part is that they were not necessarily upset because they weren't chosen. They were angry because they were still slaves to the validation and love of those who had been chosen. But what surprised me most was that there were more of us who felt like this than not.

Great Granddaddy had an interesting name for them. He called them negroes. He said they were a curious sort, perpetually infatuated with their masters, as some Yiddish women had become with their Nazi tormentors during the Yuro's second war against the world, and often how the kidnapped feel once possessed by their kidnapers. He warned us to watch them voluntarily and willfully destroy their own children's minds in order to curry their master's favor.

These lost souls rallied and petitioned and had food strikes and even helped launch and supply paramilitary guerrilla offensives against the aliens to thwart the collection process. All to no avail. Those who were hid by the negro loyalists, along with those lone bands of Yuros who headed to the hills with their weapons, made it a bit difficult for the Alkebu's subterranean sensors. But none escaped. They were powerless against Alkebu minds.

When it was all over, the negroes were forced to remain with us, not their chosen people. The Alkebu placed them under our justice. We remembered not to forget their historical treachery against us, their hatred of self. There was no truth and reconciliation committee to pardon their willed treason and bless their continued pursuit of the Yuro way. There was only we Nukembas, full of remembrance and vision. But, rather than live without their beloved masters and go through the mind-changing, reprogramming process, most chose to die by their own hands. They had no desire to know self.

The conquered Yuro nation was informed that it was being taken to become the technological slave in a new home far, far away where its skills would be put to better use.   They were informed they would never again see the planet their technological "genius" had, without the proper discipline they would now receive, devastated and nearly destroyed. They were to quickly learn that their talent, their will to destroy, was to be harnessed by the Alkebu. There would be no escape. There could not be. There was nowhere to go. Worse yet, for the Yuro, if there were a place to escape to, there would be no way to get there. Alkebu ships were completely powered and navigated by their builders' minds.

To save time, Yuro doctors were pressed to surgically place implants in their people's hearts and brains so less mental energy would be wasted keeping them in their place. These monitors were also for the express purpose of keeping Yuros from venting their frustrations out on themselves and each other. The planet Alkebulan was covered by a grid of electronic pulses that monitored the implants. If deviance in thought or act was even slightly detected, the implants would be signaled to temporarily but painfully arrest the heart and brain. Interestingly, the Alkebu were to discover that even chronically enraged Yuros only had to experience two such mind and heart numbing charges before surrendering to a lifetime of willing submission. Those desperate enough quickly found out that unauthorized implant removals brought instant death since, once in place, they permanently assumed control over the functional regulation of the heart and brain.

I can still remember as a child my father proudly showing me pictures that had won him first prize in a video contest of the look on many a Yuro's face when they discovered that what they had imagined in their science fiction was coming true. You could see the despair of having their own bodies turn against them. Their greatest fears had come to realization. And, this time, no super Yuro hero or shero came to their rescue. Although for different reasons, others were now doing to them what they had done to others. My father had finally become secure in his belief that the Universe is just. My great grandmother's soul was finally at peace.

If they were not a different people and this not a different time, you would have thought from their expressions during their evacuation that you were peering into the horrified and disbelieving faces of the women and children, indigenous to the land they stole, whom the Yuros brutally mutilated, women and children brutally mutilated after watching their husbands and fathers hunted down by dogs and scalped for sport. Their expressions reminded one of the little Nukemba boys viciously sodomized by Yuro clerics in mission schools designed to break them of their minds and traditions. One could only imagine, given their arrogance, that the chosen ones' living nightmare seemed to them to come close to the savage terror experienced by hundreds of millions of Nukembas chained, destroyed, and transported to hell while futilely trying to grasp the inhumanity of their spiritless enslavers. But we knew it was not. We understood the word justice.

Great Granddaddy said that the day the last cargo of Yuros was taken away was a thoughtful day. There was no celebration until their absence was fully realized. It took a while for their absence to settle in. Only a quiet, communal conversation slowly but surely confirming that it was not a dream was heard. Now it seems almost like they've been gone forever people say. He now smiles, as he did when Great Grandmama was around. He smiles because he knows that his great, great, great grandchildren will never have to know a Yuro.

Many years have passed since that glorious day. Nothing remains but the relics in Old World museums. Lots of pictures are still there, I'm told. Of course, there is a growing debate as to whether or not the artifacts were fabricated. The latest imagery technology has been known to be used to manufacture worlds, events and people that never existed to feed the most active imaginations. Maybe the New Nukemba School of thought is correct. Maybe they never had really occupied this planet. Maybe they were just a myth to keep us from straying onto the wrong path.

Before leaving, the Alkebu earnestly apologized to us. They let us know just how deeply it hurt them to conceal their love from us, their family, for so long. They could not trust our mentacide or imaginings until their mission was completed. Smiling ever so gently, they said they were afraid to divulge their intent to us because they were not sure if we remembered who we were. They were unsure as to whether or not we would run to warn the Yuros. Regret was also publicly expressed for taking away some of the planet's better mechanical-oriented minds. But experience had taught them that we would fully recover from the loss. However, they also said that they had witnessed our true ourstorical record and knew that we could now, as one people at peace with each other and their world, learn from our mistakes and rebuild, modeling the successes and way of our and their ancestor's humanity.

In the meantime, they left several surveillance satellites orbiting our planet to signal them if other Yuros roving the universe searching for easy prey approached us. If so, they promised to return to test out whatever new military technology their Yuros had developed for them.

Our people began the slow process of remaking the world with healing technologies, mindful of what becoming the masters of destructive technologies could bring. There was no fear that our enemies would return. But we had always been a wise people, even before our fall. And we had always listened to and honored our prophets. So, we passed Great Grandmama's counsel down to the children, keeping our eyes to the sky and plasma dischargers fully charged, just in case the Alkebu arrived a little late.

Akoben House Order Form

Please send:

_____ copies of *Battle Plan* ($12.95 each)	$ _____
_____ copies of *Eureason* ($18.95 each)	$ _____
_____ copies of *Higher Ideals* ($16.95 each)	$ _____
_____ copies of *Kebuka!* ($14.95 each)	$ _____
_____ copies of *Mentacide* ($16.95 each)	$ _____
_____ copies of *Asafo* ($16.95 each)	$ _____
_____ copies of *Complementarity* ($12.95 each)	$ _____
_____ copies of *Homosexuality and the Effeminization of Afrikan Males* ($19.95 each)	$ _____
_____ copies of *The Sex Imperative* ($16.00 each)	$ _____
_____ copies of *Excuses, Excuses* ($13.00 each)	$ _____
_____ copies of *negroes and other essays* ($13.00 each)	$ _____
_____ copies of *Chess Primer* ($12.95 each)	$ _____

Shipping & Handling: $ _____
($4 for 1 book and $2 for each additional book.)

TOTAL ENCLOSED: $ _____

NAME: _____

ADDRESS: _____

_____

E-mail (Optional): _____

Send this order form, along with your check or money order (<u>made payable to LARRY CRAWFORD</u>), to:

Akoben House, P.O. Box 10786, Atlanta, GA 30310

or order by credit card at

www.AkobenHouse.com